THE GRASSHOPPER

REINALDO DOMINGOS

AUTHOR
REINALDO DOMINGOS

ILLUSTRATION
TANIA RICCI

INTERNATIONAL EDITORIAL DIRECTOR
ANDRÉ L. PASOTTO

EDITORIAL COORDINATOR
RENATA DE SÁ

ENGLISH VERSION
ANA MILITELLO

ART TEXT
BRUNO LEITE

ART EDITOR
MAURO ROBERTO FERNANDES

Dados Internacionais de Catalogação na Publicação (CIP)
(Câmara Brasileira do Livro, SP, Brasil)

Domingos, Reinaldo
The grasshopper / Reinaldo Domingos ; ilustração Tania Ricci ; tradução Ana Militello. -- 1. ed. -- São Paulo : Editora DSOP, 2020. -- (Explorer ; 1)

Título original: The grasshopper
ISBN 978-65-87565-15-6

1. Sonhos - Literatura infantojuvenil I. Ricci, Tania. II. Militello, Ana. III. Título IV. Série.

20-46368 CDD-028.5

Índices para catálogo sistemático:

1. Literatura infantojuvenil 028.5

Aline Graziele Benitez - Bibliotecária - CRB-1/3129

DEAR READER,

MY NAME IS REINALDO, AND JUST LIKE YOU, I WAS ONCE A CHILD. SINCE I WAS LITTLE, I LOVED TO INVENT STORIES AND CREATE IMAGINARY WORLDS. AS I GREW UP, MY BIGGEST DREAM WAS TO SHARE MY STORIES WITH CHILDREN WORLDWIDE.

MY DREAM CAME TRUE. YOU HAVE THE ABILITY TO ACHIEVE YOUR DREAMS TOO. ALL YOU NEED TO DO IS FOLLOW THE FOUR STEPS OF THE METHODOLOGY I CREATED, WHICH YOU WILL LEARN IN THIS BOOK.

BESIDES HELPING YOU TO MAKE YOUR DREAMS COME TRUE, I WANT TO INVITE YOU TO TAKE PART IN THIS STORY WITH ME – BY PAINTING AND DRAWING...

I HOPE YOU ENJOY IT!

ALL THE BEST,

REINALDO DOMINGOS

"FOR CHILDREN ALL OVER THE WORLD WHO CAN

BUILD A FUTURE WITH BALANCE AND HARMONY."

Reinaldo Domingos

ONCE UPON A TIME, THERE WAS A SMALL BOY CALLED NICO, AN ANT AND A GRASSHOPPER.

THEY LIVED IN THE SAME PLACE, BUT THEY DIDN'T KNOW EACH OTHER. NICO LIVED IN THE HOUSE. THE ANT AND THE GRASSHOPPER LIVED IN THE GARDEN.

THEY ALL LIVED IN THEIR OWN WORLD; ONE HERE, ONE THERE, AND NICO FARTHER AWAY.

1 LOOK AND POINT. WHERE DO THEY LIVE (NICO, ANT AND GRASSHOPPER)?

THE ANT WORKED HARDER THAN ANYONE ELSE IN THE GARDEN. EVERY DAY SHE CARRIED OUT LEAVES ON HER BACK TO HER HOME.

SHE LIVED IN A WORLD WITH AN ENORMOUS GARDEN FULL OF LEAVES, GRAINS AND FRUIT.

THE ANT BELIEVED THAT WORK WAS THE MOST IMPORTANT THING IN THE WORLD.

THE GRASSHOPPER ENTERTAINED EVERYONE IN THE GARDEN. HE PLAYED HIS GUITAR AND SANG NIGHT AND DAY WITH HIS BEAUTIFUL VOICE; HE DIDN'T WANT TO WORK.

HIS WORLD WAS LIKE AN ORCHESTRA, FULL OF MUSICAL NOTES AND MELODIES TO TRY OUT HERE, THERE AND EVERYWHERE.

FOR THE GRASSHOPPER, MUSIC WAS THE MOST IMPORTANT THING IN THE WORLD.

2 CONNECT THE ANT AND THE GRASSHOPPER TO THE OBJECTS.

NICO HAD MORE WISHES THAN THE ANT AND THE GRASSHOPPER. HE SPENT HIS DAYS DREAMING ABOUT THINGS HE WOULD LIKE TO HAVE.

HE KNEW THAT TO MAKE HIS DREAMS COME TRUE, HE NEEDED MONEY. FOR NICO, MONEY WAS THE MOST IMPORTANT THING IN THE WORLD.

3 CIRCLE WHAT IS IMPORTANT TO THEM.

ONE EVENING BEFORE GOING TO SLEEP, THE ANT, THE GRASSHOPPER AND NICO ALL LISTENED TO A LOVELY STORY HIS MOTHER DECIDED TO TELL HER SON.

THE GRASSHOPPER SPENT THE SUMMER SINGING HAPPILY TO EVERYONE, BUT, IN THE WINTER, HE WAS POOR.

THE WEATHER WAS COLD AND THE GRASSHOPPER DIDN'T STORE ANY FOOD.

WITH NOTHING TO EAT, THE GRASSHOPPER DECIDED TO VISIT THE ANT WHO LIVED NEAR HIM.

THE GRASSHOPPER ASKED THE ANT TO GIVE HIM SOME GRAINS, TO SURVIVE UNTIL THE SUMMER.

– I WILL GIVE IT BACK TO YOU – SAID THE GRASSHOPPER.

– I GIVE YOU MY WORD. I WILL PAY YOU BACK FOR THE FOOD WITH INTEREST.

THE ANT, PUT HER HANDS ON HER HIPS AND ASKED ANGRILY.

– WHAT DID YOU DO ALL SUMMER LONG?

– NIGHT AND DAY, I SANG HAPPILY – SAID THE GRASSHOPPER.

– BUT IT IS WINTER NOW, AND I CAN'T SING IN THE COLD – SAID THE GRASSHOPPER.

– AH, HOW LOVELY! – MOCKED THE ANT.

– YOU SANG? WELL, YOU CAN DANCE NOW!

4 NUMBER THE SCENES FROM THE ANT AND THE GRASSHOPPER STORY. THEN COLOR.

AFTER LISTENING TO HIS MOM TELLING THE STORY, NICO WAS STUNNED WITH ALL THE UNFAMILIAR WORDS AND SOUNDS HE HEARD.

HE WONDERED IF IN THE WORLD OF ANTS AND GRASSHOPPERS, PERHAPS THIS WAS A COMMON WAY OF SPEAKING TO EACH OTHER.

AFTER THINKING ABOUT THE STORY, NICO HAD MIXED FEELINGS ABOUT IT.

HE WAS FEELING SORRY FOR THE GRASSHOPPER BECAUSE HE HAD NO FOOD TO EAT. HE WAS ALONE IN THE COLD AND WINDY WEATHER.

BUT HE ALSO FELT SORRY FOR THE ANT, BECAUSE DURING THE SUMMER, SHE WORKED HARD COLLECTING FOOD FOR HER ANTHILL.

NICO ASKED HIS MOM:

– WHO IS RIGHT IN THIS STORY?

SHE SAID:

– YOU ALREADY KNOW THE ANSWER TO THAT QUESTION, SON.

THINK ABOUT IT.

NICO THOUGHT ABOUT THE STORY FOR A LONG TIME, WHEN THE ANSWER CAME TO HIM.

THE GRASSHOPPER REMINDED HIM OF HIS MOM SINGING ALL DAY, HERE AND THERE.

AND THE ANT REMINDED HIM OF HIS DAD, WHO WORKED HARD AS A TRAIN ENGINEER. HE WAS ALWAYS OPERATING THE TRAIN CARS IN THE SUN, IN THE RAIN, IN THE COLD AND IN THE WIND.

5 MATCH THE CHARACTERS.

SUDDENLY NICO REALIZED THAT HIS MOM AND DAD HAD DIFFERENT WAYS OF DOING THINGS. SOMETIMES THEIR WAYS OF DOING THINGS BLENDED WITH ONE ANOTHER.

HIS DAD WOULD PLAY SONGS ON HIS GUITAR SITTING ON THE SOFA, VERY HAPPY AND RELAXED.

HIS MOM WORKED HARD TO CLEAN THE HOUSE AND KEEP THINGS NEAT AND SPOTLESS.

SHE DIDN'T REST, SHE WAS ALWAYS FOCUSED AND QUIET!

AFTER DOING SO MUCH THINKING, NICO WAS TIRED. HE FELL ASLEEP AND DREAMED OF AN ENORMOUS SEESAW.

ON ONE SIDE OF THIS SEESAW, SAT THE ANT. ON THE OTHER SIDE, SAT THE GRASSHOPPER. WHEN NICO WOKE UP, HE HAD THE ANSWER HE WAS LOOKING FOR.

6 PAINT THE MEDIUM SEESAW AND COMPLETE THE WORDS.

EN__R__OU__

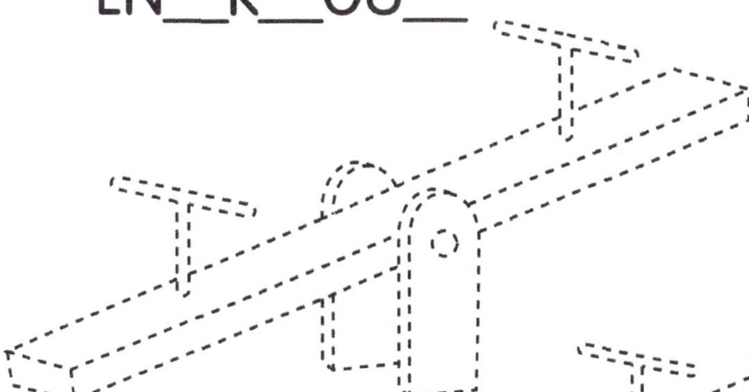

M__DIU__

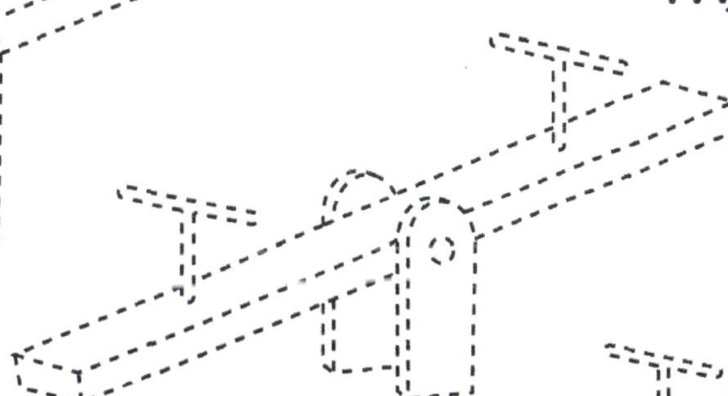

S__A__L

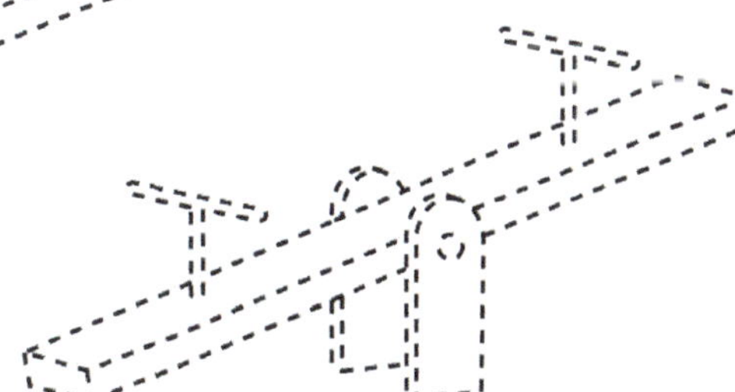

NEITHER THE ANT NOR THE GRASSHOPPER WAS RIGHT.

A PERFECT SOLUTION FOR THIS PROBLEM, ANTHOPPERS!

IF THE ANT PLAYED A LITTLE AND THE GRASSHOPPER WORKED A LITTLE,

EVERYTHING WOULD BE FINE IN THE END.

7 CIRCLE NICO'S DREAM IN THE STORY.

FROM THAT DAY ON, NICO LEARNED ABOUT BALANCE.

LIKE A SEESAW, EVERYTHING IN LIFE HAS TWO SIDES. MOST OF THE TIME, THERE IS BALANCE BETWEEN TWO THINGS.

THE RULE APPLIES TO WORK AND REST OR STUDY AND PLAY.

IT ALSO APPLIES TO MONEY.

8 DRAW ACTIVITIES YOU LIKE TO DO THAT...

NEED SOME MONEY.

DON'T NEED ANY MONEY.

NICO DISCOVERED THAT MONEY ISN'T THE MOST IMPORTANT THING IN THE WORLD.

MONEY IS ONLY A SMALL PART OF A GREATER WORLD. THE WORLD ALSO HAS LEAVES, GRASSHOPPERS SINGING, BIRDS BUILDING NESTS, MOTHERS SINGING IN THE LIVING ROOM AND FATHERS PLAYING THEIR GUITAR ON THE SOFA.

FINALLY, NICO LEARNED HOW IMPORTANT A BALANCED LIFE IS TO MAKE DREAMS COME TRUE AND LIVE HAPPILY.

9 AFTER READING THE STORY AND LEARNING THAT IN LIFE IT IS NECESSARY TO HAVE BALANCE TO MAKE YOUR MATERIAL AND NON-MATERIAL DREAMS COME TRUE.

DRAW ONE MATERIAL DREAM.

DRAW ONE NON-MATERIAL DREAM.

10 PAINT AND CUT-OUT THE CHARACTERS. THEN RETELL THE STORY.

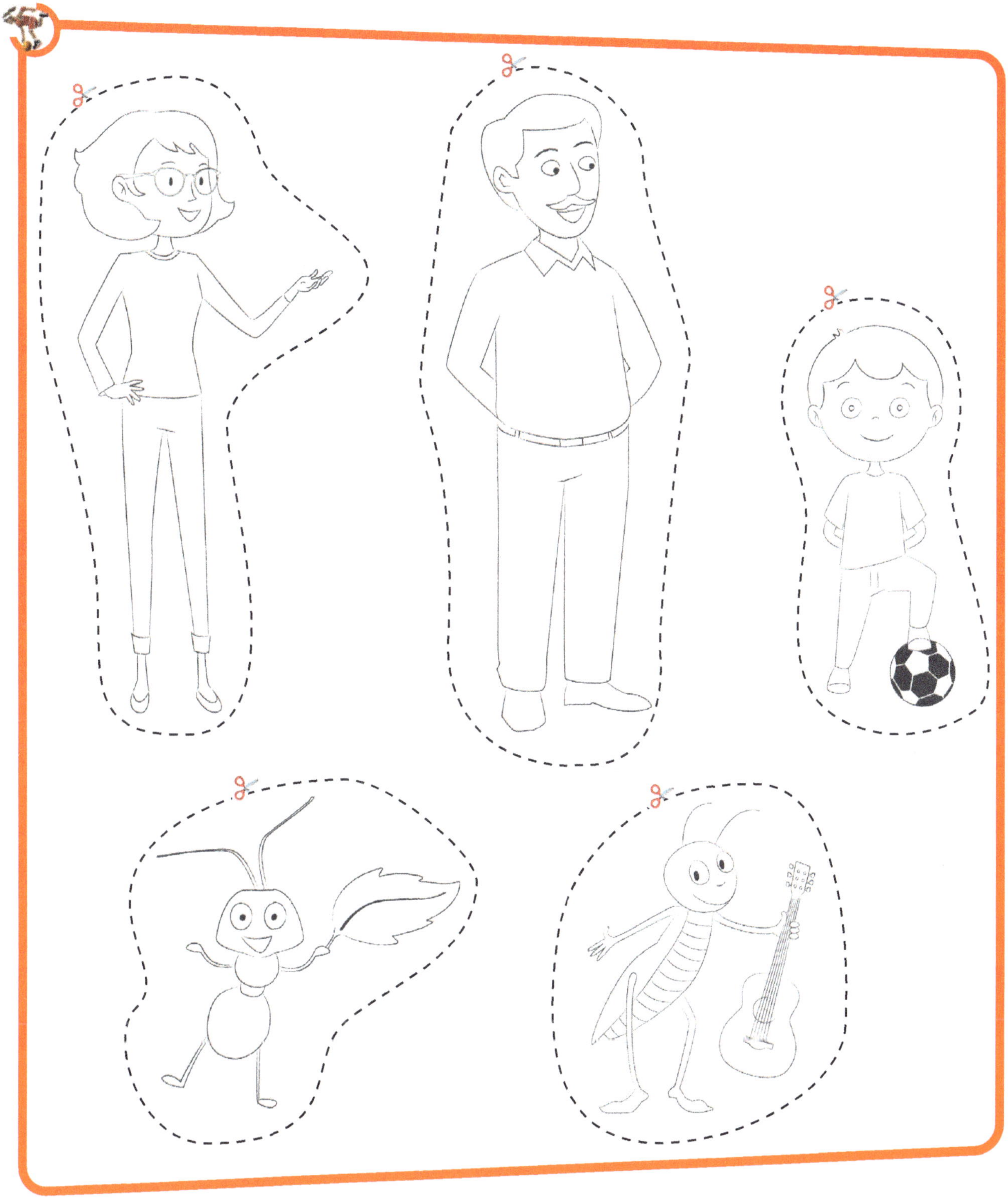

THE GRASSHOPPER

A VERY SPECIAL MESSAGE FROM DSOP

To the teachers or parents/ guardians

Congratulations, you just took the first step towards an investment with an invaluable return: prosperity, in every moment of your family's life, beginning with your young student!

The **DSOP Methodology** illustrates how important it is to have dreams in our lives, and above all how to achieve them. It focuses upon behavioural development, with the goal of creating a healthier financial life. This makes it possible to build a life filled with accomplishments.

The DSOP books, courses and educational programmes for children and young people also include content which extends to family members and school staff. The guidance given, both in the manuals and projects offered to teachers and from the DSOP advisors and pedagogical support team, will help your young student to transform their life, inspired by the captivating and entrepreneurial paths taken by the characters in the stories.

There is growing awareness internationally of the importance of incorporating Financial Education in school curriculums. In some cases, this is combined with teaching students to develop conscious behaviour around consumption practices. The UN proposed the 17 Sustainable Development Goals (SNGs) and included **Responsible**

MENSAGEM MUITO ESPECIAL DA DSOP

Aos responsáveis pelos alunos ou seus familiares

Parabéns, você acaba de dar o primeiro passo rumo a um investimento de retorno inestimável: a prosperidade em todos os momentos da vida da sua família, começando pelo jovem estudante da sua casa!

A **Metodologia DSOP** mostra a importância dos sonhos em nossas vidas e, especialmente, como alcançá-los. O foco está no desenvolvimento comportamental para uma vida financeira mais saudável. Assim, é possível construir uma vida cheia de realizações.

Os livros, cursos e programas educacionais para crianças e jovens também são complementados por conteúdos que se estendem à sua família e funcionários da escola. Com o apoio das orientações dos manuais e projetos oferecidos aos professores e da assessoria e suporte pedagógicos da DSOP, eles ajudarão o jovem estudante a transformar a vida inspirado nas adoráveis trajetórias empreendedoras das personagens.

A BNCC (Base Nacional Comum Curricular) tornou obrigatório nas escolas públicas e privadas o ensino de Educação Financeira nos Anos Iniciais e Finais do Ensino Fundamental, porém voltado para que os alunos desenvolvam um comportamento de consumo consciente.
A própria ONU propõe os 17 Objetivos de Sustentabilidade

MENSAJE MUY ESPECIAL DE DSOP

A las familias de los alumnos o sus responsables

¡Felicitaciones! Usted acaba de dar el primer paso rumbo a una inversión de valor inestimable: la prosperidad en todos los momentos de la vida de su familia, empezando por los jóvenes estudiantes de su casa.

La **Metodología DSOP** potencia la valoración de los sueños en nuestras vidas y, especialmente, cómo alcanzarlos. El énfasis está en el desarrollo comportamental hacia una vida financiera más saludable, pues así es posible construir una vida de realizaciones. Los libros, cursos y programas educacionales para jóvenes son también complementados por contenidos que alcanzan a sus familias y toda la comunidad escolar.

Con el apoyo de las orientaciones de los manuales, proyectos, asesoría y soporte pedagógicos de la Editorial DSOP, los profesores ayudarán a su joven estudiante a transformar su vida, inspirado en las adorables trayectorias emprendedoras de los personajes.

En Brasil hay leyes que han vuelto obligatoria en las escuelas públicas y privadas la enseñanza de la Educación Financiera volcada hacia el desarrollo de un comportamiento de consumo consciente. La misma ONU propone 17 Objetivos de Sustentabilidad para la Humanidad e incluye **Consumption**, refiriéndose exactamente a esa cuestión.

Consumption, referring to precisely this objective.

For over 10 years, Reinaldo Domingos PhD has been sharing his methodology with the world via the DSOP group. It has brought great success not only for him, but also for all the Financial Educators and Financial Therapists who have graduated during this decade, as well as, more recently, through franchises. Its efficiency has been proven not only in practice, but also by the academic and scientific world; his methodology has been championed in the United States at universally commended master, doctoral and post-doctoral levels.

When it comes to behaviour, the best way to develop it swiftly and achieve efficient results is to start as early as possible and maintain consistency. We need to begin preparing ourselves for adult life in childhood, and by doing so we can achieve financial independence earlier than previous generations, and dedicate our efforts and time towards realising our own dreams and those of the people we love.

So, how does this transformational methodology work? Learn more and win a free e-book on *DSOP Financial Education Methodology*, visit the link or QR Code on the back cover of this book.

para a Humanidade e incluiu o **Consumption**, referindo-se exatamente a esse objetivo.

Há mais de 10 anos, por meio do Grupo DSOP, o PhD Reinaldo Domingos tem compartilhado com o mundo sua metodologia vivenciada com sucesso não só por ele, como também por todos os Educadores Financeiros e Terapeutas Financeiros formados ao longo dessa década, além do trabalho mais recente com os franqueados. Não só a prática comprovou sua eficiência, mas também o mundo acadêmico e científico, pois sua metodologia também foi defendida nos Estados Unidos em níveis de mestrado, doutorado e pós-doutorado aprovados com louvor e de forma unânime.

Quando falamos de comportamento, a melhor maneira de desenvolvê-lo rapidamente rumo aos resultados eficientes, é começando o quanto antes e mantendo a continuidade. Desde criança, temos que nos preparar para a vida adulta; assim, poderemos nos tornar independentes mais cedo que as gerações anteriores e direcionar nossos esforços e tempo, a partir de então, para a realização de sonhos próprios e os de quem amamos.

Mas, como é essa metodologia transformadora? Saiba mais e ganhe um e-book sobre a *Metodologia DSOP de Educação Financeira*, por meio do QR Code atrás deste livro.

Hace más de 10 años, por medio del Grupo DSOP, el PHD Reinaldo Domingos ha compartido su metodología vivenciada con éxito no solo por él sino por todos los Educadores Financieros y Terapeutas financieros formados en sus cursos. Además de toda la comprobación práctica, está también el reconocimiento académico y científico, pues la Metodología DSOP ha sido defendida en los EEUU en niveles de máster, de doctorado y posdoctorado.

Cuando se trata de comportamiento, para garantizar resultados eficientes en el futuro, lo mejor es desarrollarlo lo más pronto posible, además de mantener su continuidad. Desde niños, debemos ir preparándonos para los principales retos de la vida adulta, para volvernos independientes financieramente aún antes de la edad en la que las generaciones anteriores lo lograban. Así, podremos concentrarnos a partir de entonces no solo en disfrutar de los sueños ya alcanzados, sino también a multiplicarlos e incluir a quienes amamos en esa trayectoria.

Pero, ¿cómo es esa metodología transformadora? Para saberlo, infórmese mejor y adquiera su e-book sobre Educación Financiera en el código QR detrás de este libro.